MY LIFE AS A STALINIST

My Life As A Stalinist

Gerry Murphy

SOUTHWORDeditions

First published in 2018
by Southword Editions
The Munster Literature Centre
Frank O'Connor House, 84 Douglas Street
Cork, Ireland

Set in Adobe Caslon 12pt
Printed by City Print Cork, Ireland

Contents

for Sean Murphy, Marian Keating & Michael Buckley

*"And one thing, therefore, can never be made good:
having neglected to run away from home."*

- Walter Benjamin

An age since
a faltering dray-horse
kicked my grandfather's
lights out on Blackpool Bridge
and left him groping
for meaning and connection
in the Asylum.
An age before
I stumbled into verse,
raving blessedly
between truth and delusion
to the sound of Pegasus'
approaching hooves.

Oh For Fucksake

The terry-cloth nappy
is cold, wet and full.
I am three-months-old
and already into my first,
all-singing, all-dancing,
existential crisis.

And it's only 1953!

Learning At My Grandmother's Knee

"If you don't behave,
I'll redden the poker in the fire,
take down your pants
and make a Freemason of you,"
warned my grandmother.
How this was to be carried out –
not being sure of my grandmother's
familiarity with the obscure
initiation rites of the Freemasons –
I had no idea,
being only seven-years-old
at the time.
But I knew enough to know,
that it would be swift, brutal
and extremely painful.
So, I behaved.

Epitaph for an Old I.R.A. Man

That gas-pipe baluba, my grandfather,
has blown his last dart
into the stratosphere.
We found him grinning
under the wheels of the Royal Carriage
this morning,
his un-exploded corgi-bomb
pressed to a jelly.

School's Out
(for Mick & Ted Noonan)

Three days after the Senior Infants
got their Summer holidays,
the Junior Infants were let loose.
It had been raining heavily
all that morning and the streets
were slick and dotted with puddles.
We, the Noonan twins and me,
must have hit every single one,
smack-dab in the middle,
leaping and splashing and squealing
in a wild exhilarating dance,
all the way home to our aghast mothers,
who could scarcely recognise
our mud-spattered faces,
our beaming grins.

Running Away From Home

I have been playing all afternoon
with my brother and sister,
during which I have managed
to upset one of our neighbours
by running through his rose garden.
He threatens to inform my mother,
no need, my brother and sister
are already running home to tell her.
When I get to the front gate,
I can see they have told her everything.
"Wait till I get you inside,"
she calls from the front door.
From the top of the steps
I make my announcement:
"I'm running away from home
and I'm never coming back!"
"Off you go," she replies.
"Don't forget to write,"
she calls after me
as I take to my heels.
About fifty yards from the house,
on the hill leading down
to the main road,
the presbytery looms
in the gathering darkness,
its stand of cypress trees
soughing and creaking
in a freshening breeze.
Daunted, I turn tail
and run back home.
When I knock on the front door
my mother answers.
"You didn't get far and you never wrote,"
she says.
My promised beating forgotten
in her helpless laughter.

"Stop kicking the stones,
you'll scuff your new shoes!"
We are on our way home from Mass
and I am trying to score the winning goal
in the always running
world-cup-final in my head
with every loose stone on the hill
leading up from the chapel.
My last shot,
screaming into the top-left corner
of the English net,
almost clipping the wing-mirror
of the long black limousine,
gliding past in a solemn hush,
upon which my father loses it:
"Now look what you nearly did,
are you trying to get us into trouble
with the Church?"
"Have you any idea who that is?"
From his plush leather seat,
the Bishop smiles and waves,
waves and smiles.

Oh Ronnie Delaney

"Will you go down to the shop
and get the Echo, a half-pound of sausages
and a pint of milk,"
my father asks.
"But it's not my turn, I went yesterday,"
I wail.
"Ah go on, we'll time you,"
my mother promises.
I take off like a greyhound,
streaking down the hill,
hurtling past Father Lynch,
who shouts: "On the clock?"
"Yes, I gasp in reply
and surge into top gear.
I tumble into Rodgers' shop,
get the messages on the "book"
and start back up the hill.
Back in the house,
out of breath,
in a lather of sweat,
I manage to wheeze at my mother:
"Time?"
"Time?" she replies.

Cannibal

The first time
I tasted human flesh,
I was ten-years-old.
It happened during an argument
with my twelve-year-old brother,
in which he dismissed
my beloved Beatles
as overblown, overplayed
and strictly for cretins.
I lost the plot,
fastened onto him
and took a sizeable chunk
of flesh from his shoulder,
a piece of which
(probably gristle)
got stuck in my teeth.
Howling and gnashing ensued
until my mother intervened.
She was so shocked
at what I had done,
she clean forgot to beat me
and sent me straight to bed
without my supper.
But hey, I had already eaten.

Pups

Sent to bed early,
my brother and me,
our giddy horseplay upsetting
our grandmother's annual visit,
while our well-behaved sister is allowed
to stay up and listen to the fascinating tales
our grandmother usually relates,
we are bored, resentful and restless
and it's still bright outside.
The horseplay starts up again,
we begin to wrestle, trying to pin
each other down into the rumpled sheets,
grappling, twisting and grunting until
we tumble out of bed and slam
onto the floor with a ceiling-testing crash.
Our grandmother, convinced that the Black & Tans
have returned, starts raving about "the guns in the attic,
they'll find the guns in the attic and murder us all,"
upon which my father, who has warned us twice already,
comes thundering up the stairs,
grabbing the dog's leash on his way.
"You nearly gave your grandmother a heart-attack
with all your caffling," he roars,
as we turn over and under each other,
trying in vain to avoid the flailing leash,
yelping and wailing and howling.

Annual Anabasis

In the Woodford Bourne van,
Danny driving, my father up front.
My mother, brother, sister and me,
packed in the back
and swaying giddily from side
to side with the holiday gear.
On our way to Graball Bay
for two weeks in my Aunt's
moth-haunted, ramshackle bungalow.
Excitement building since Douglas,
bubbling over at Carrigaline,
and as we rounded the bend at Drake's Pool,
holding on to each other for dear life,
we knew we would shortly
get our first teasing glimpse
of the yacht-bedecked sea at Crosshaven.
Upon which we would cry out in unison,
like the Ten Thousand on Mount Theches:
"Thálatta!" "Thálatta" "Thalatta!"

Not long after
the Tooth Fairy stopped
leaving shiny new pennies
under my pillow,
the Angel of Death,
gathering my mother
into his huge beating wings,
shook a dusty black feather
onto my bed.

Six months after
the report of your death,
I start a rumour among my schoolmates
that you are still alive.
That you are hiding out
in the Bolivian Andes
with a Lt. Colonel of the Treasury Brigade
who fled La Paz during one of three
October coups d'état
with thirty million U.S. dollars
and four lorry-loads of gold.

Just wait for the letters,
I tell them,
and the postal orders.

Nothing Is Lost
(after Randall Jarrell)

As if my mother
stepped from the shuffling throng
on South Main Street
and stood before me:
"Dead? Who told you I was dead?"

My Father Drying My Hair

I have washed my hair
and I am drying it
somewhat distractedly
by the fire.
"Dry it properly,"
my father commands
from behind his newspaper.
I make a half-hearted attempt
but soon lapse into ineffectual dabbing
at its dripping ends.
Eventually, as is his wont,
he takes the towel
and vigorously rubs it dry.
My head, held sweetly
in the busy orbit of his hands,
lulled into a drowsy rapture.

My Life As A Stalinist

"Capitalist Lackey!"
I shout at my father across the dinner table,
during a discussion on the feasibility
of the Second Five Year Plan,
the return of Fianna Fáil to government,
or my dismal school report,
probably all three.
The conversation stutters to a halt
and for a moment there is silence.
My father's response is laughter,
knowing full-well that I am only half-aware
of the meaning of my misdirected insult.
"You're a great one for the slogans, Gerry boy,
try to read a little more
of the literature underpinning them."
"In fact, go back to your beloved Stalin
and study his voluminous essays
on this very subject and his methods of dealing
with 'back-sliders', 'saboteurs' and 'lackeys',
then get back to me
and call me whatever you like."

The Secret Life of My Father

They would meet,
Mr. Broderick and my father
(solid Sunday morning choir men)
to play their records,
on alternating Friday nights
in each other's sitting rooms.
Discussing the relative merits
of Gigli and McCormack,
Callas and Sutherland,
Bjorling and Wunderlich.
Comfortable in their slippers,
they would skin-up and roll
two thick joints of Colombian Gold
and kick back
to the opening bars
of Haydn's "Creation".

BREAKTHROUGH

Mexico, 1970.
World Cup, quarter final.
England, two up against West Germany
and cruising.
My brother, quietly gloating,
my father and I plunged
into glum, staring silence.
I go out into the kitchen
to make tea,
West Germany claw one back.
"Too little, too late,"
my brother declares.
I go back into the kitchen,
West Germany equalise.
My father and I are led out
blinking, into the daylight.

In extra-time,
Muller, "Der Bomber" scores the winner.
I had never hugged my father,
I haven't hugged him since.

A Question for Mick Murphy

I wonder if you had lived longer
would you have gone to America,
to watch the "home runs"
streak out over the cheering stands,
rather than hanging on desperately
to an oscillating signal from the wireless,
carrying DiMaggio's magic
clear across the Atlantic?

My Dead Father Reading Over My Shoulder

Madrid. Late November.
Mid-morning on the Plaza Cibeles
under a newly-installed, blue-tinted,
plate-glass sky.
Coffee, croissants and the Herald Tribune,
simple empire of the moment.
The café's one-eyed cat
calm among the pigeons
as frantic shoals of traffic
anxiously negotiate the Square.

Light on the Paseo del Prado,
light on the page
as I drowsily scan a report
on the World Series:
"first base", "pinch hit", "home run",
phrases floating out past my ken
as if being read by someone else.

Buy your own paper, father.

HOLY SOULS

November:
here's the ghost of my mother
on her way down to early Mass
followed by the ghost
of her favourite cat
who will wait,
watching for poor ghost mice
from the door of the church,
then follow her
back up the hill
to where the ghost of my father
is preparing breakfast for two
while their real children
sleep fitfully on.

Why I am a Poet

Is it all down to my father's habit
of smoking Sweet Afton cigarettes
and my reading and re-reading
Burns' lovely couplet on the packet:
"Flow gently sweet Afton amang thy green braes,
flow gently I'll sing thee a song in thy praise."
Was it my uncle Paddy soaring
on those kite-like tropes of Omar Khayyám
between gulps of mulled porter?
Or my mother squirreling away
those hurriedly scribbled notes
beneath the sofa cushions,
which I would often find
but could never quite get,
verses from her own lost Rubáiyát?

On His Deathbed My Grandfather Warns Me Against Literature

"Books!"
snarled my grandfather,
"are a bloodless substitute for life."
The thick blue ink of his veins
clotting happily
into commas, semi-colons
and colons,
towards a sudden and glorious
full stop.

Acknowledgements

Some of these poem have appeared in previous collections, namely, *End of Part One*, Dedalus Press 2006, *My Flirtation With International Socialism*, Dedalus Press 2010 and *Muse*, Dedalus Press 2015. My thanks to the Editor of Dedalus Press, Pat Boran. Some have also appeared in journals, namely *Cuirt Journal 2004, The Irish Times, The Irish Examiner* and the anthology *Reading The Future*, Arlen House, 2018.